Getting dressed for COSTUME PARTY

STICKER ACTIVITY BOOK

Om KIDZ
An imprint of Om Books International

It is Ana's birthday and she is going to celebrate it with all her friends. Help her and Susie get dressed in time for the costume party!

Here's Rosy and Pam getting ready for the party. What should they wear to look like a fairy and a clown?

Sam and James are being creative with their costumes - one is going to be a caterpillar, the other a butterfly!

Now it's your turn to be creative
and dress them up.

Kiara wants to dress up as a bunny and Tom as a carrot. What should they wear?

Pg 2
Pg 3
Pg 4
Pg 5

Pg 6

Pg 7

Pg 8

Pg 9

Pg 10

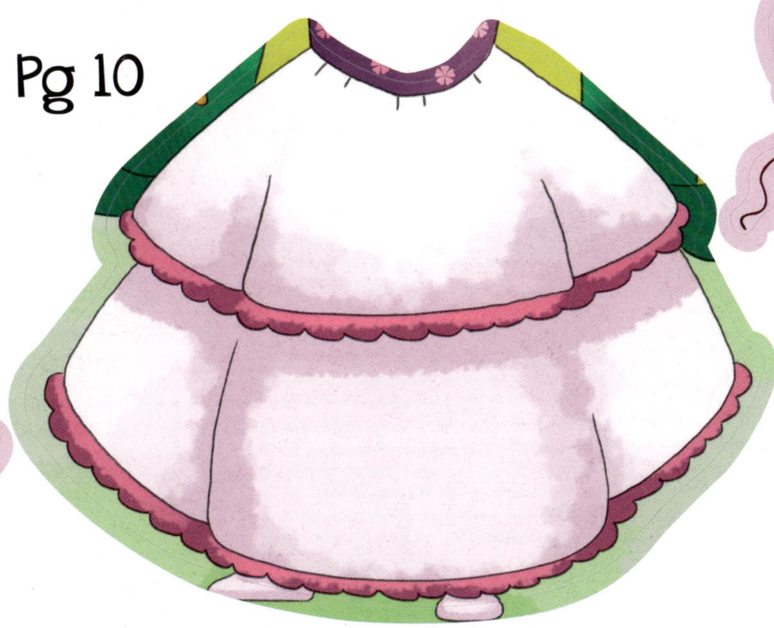
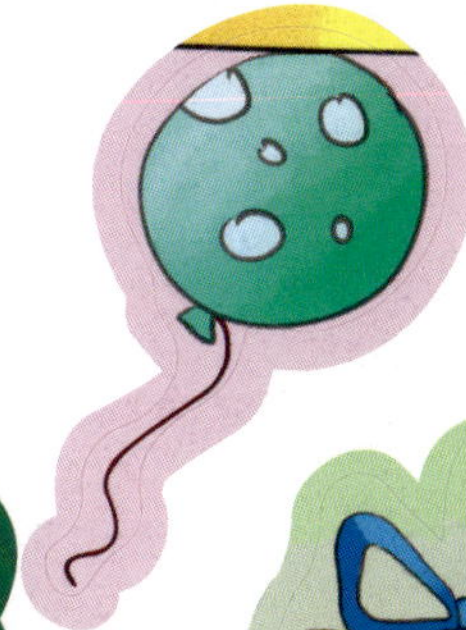

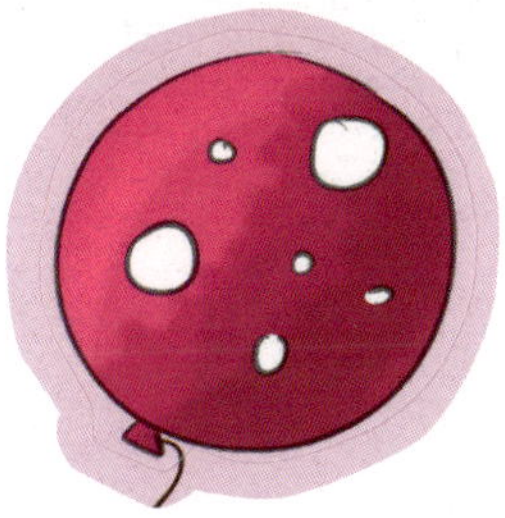

Pg 11

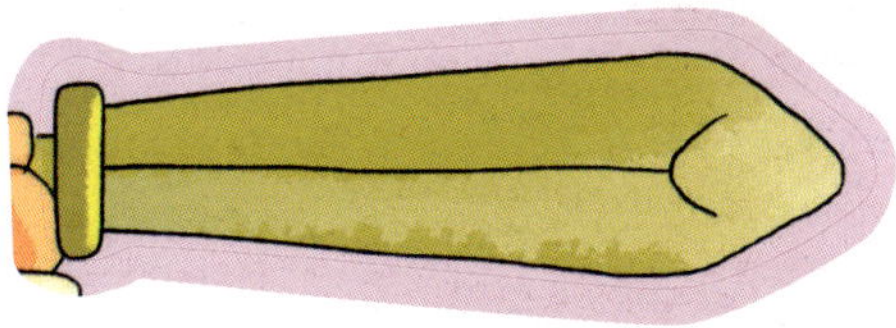

Pg 12

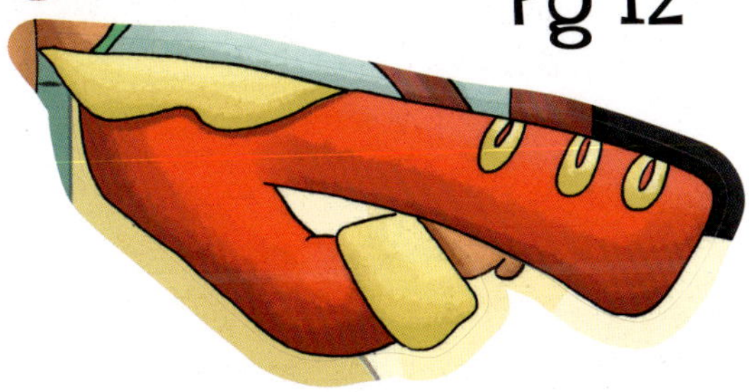
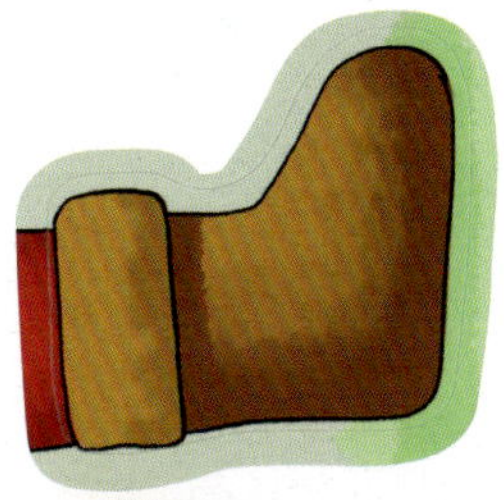
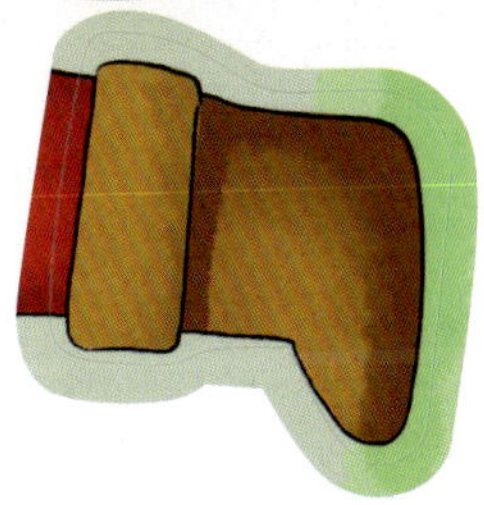
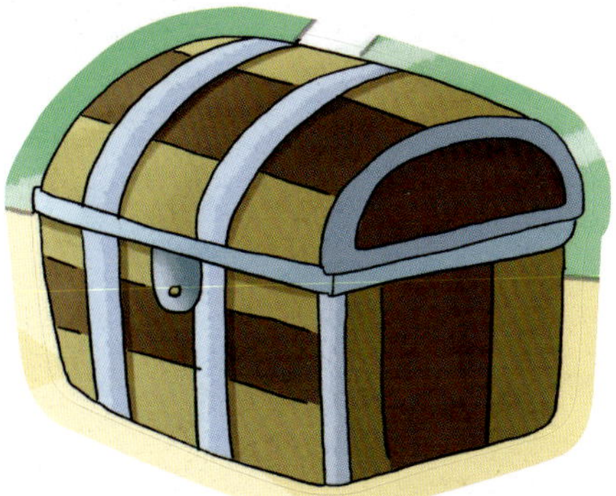
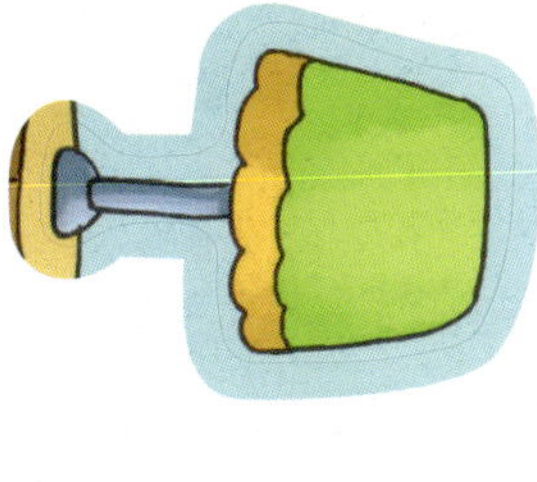
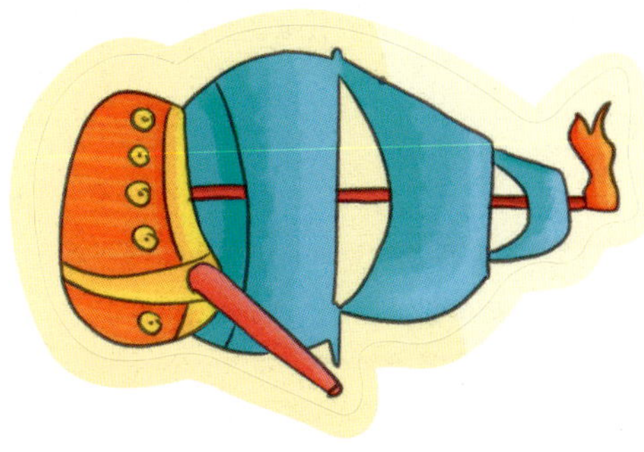

Pg 13

Pg 14

Pg 15

Pg 16

Miranda and Bob have decided to become the characters of a fairytale.

Dress up Bob as a prince and
Miranda as the princess!

And here's Samuel, the pirate, and Oliver, the superhero, ready to play their parts. Touch up their costumes with your stickers.

What are Kim and Kate dressed as?
Paste the stickers to find out!

Isn't it exciting to be dressed as a snowman? Dress up Rosh so that he dosen't miss out on the fun!